Career Transition

B. Vincent

Published by RWG Publishing, 2021.

CAREER TRANSITION

First edition. June 8, 2021.

Written by B. Vincent.

Also by B. Vincent

Affiliate Marketing
Affiliate Marketing

Standalone
Affiliate Recruiting
Business Layoffs & Firings
Business and Entrepreneur Guide
Business Remote Workforce
Career Transition

Career Transition

STEVE JOBS ONCE SAID the only way to do great work is to love what you do. If you haven't found it yet, keep looking, don't settle. And Andre Gide tells us, man cannot discover new oceans, unless he has the courage to lose sight of the shore. Career transition can be one of the scariest things you'll ever face. Sometimes it's foisted on in the form of a layoff or a business failure. Sometimes it's a profound voluntary decision you force yourself to make. In either case, the fear of the unknown, the stress of transition, and the very real risk of failure are enough to discourage anyone caught in such a situation, and yet a career transition whether forced or voluntary can often be one of the most rewarding and positive events in a person's life. So, how do we optimize this turning of the page, how do we ensure we approach this next chapter of our lives with optimism, enthusiasm, and drive. In this course, we'll show you how to do exactly that.

More than 70% of the US workforce is actively looking for a change in career. 30% will probably change careers every 12 months. The average person will change careers five to seven times in their lifetime. These statistics show that career transition is an increasingly important area, that businesses should consider.

Our course is going to consist of a series of critical discussion points. These are designed to cover this broad topic as thoroughly as possible, to encourage growth in these vital areas, and to facilitate a real and fruitful discussion within your organization about how you can each improve on this essential characteristic, both at work and in your personal lives in general. Some of these will be pretty lengthy and some will be relatively straightforward and brief. At the very end of this roadmap, comes the most important final step. Discussion time do not skip this. This is the most important part of this training.

When you finish this course, you need to spend at least an hour or so, going over the questions we supply yet the end as a group, whoever's the head honcho in the group should designate a facilitator, whose responsibility it is, that each question is covered and that everyone, time permitting, is able to have their say. Make sure all contributions are valued, all suggestions considered, and all opinions respected. So, let's move into the first discussion point.

Career transition is a period of self-examination, in which you decide that it's time to move on to a new career to earn more, pursue a passion or dream, or have more time for personal and family life. From the word transition, it's obviously not an overnight thing, it's a process. In some cases, this shift can take over a year to execute. The reason is that there's a lot of planning involved. First on the list, is by identifying what would be your next potential career. To do that, you need to assess your interests and skills. Look back at your past work experiences, then ask yourself, what are their skills and expertise do I know, take a trip down memory lane and review the roles you enjoy doing in the past, including volunteer work and other activities by meditating on your past experiences, you can identify the skills you acquired, your core values and what areas you're truly inclined at.

No matter how self-sufficient you think you are, you'll eventually need help at some point. This is especially true when it comes to transitioning careers. After all, every new chapter in life will involve some challenges. Why not try hearing the thoughts of others, reach out to family, friends, and colleagues for some tips and advice. Some of them were maybe in the same shoes as you are, gain insight from people working in the field you're exploring. Learning from these people is highly advantageous, as it will help you to make the right decisions moving forward.

Another way of seeking support is by checking if your current company offers outplacement assistance. Outplacement services are designed to help employees to have a successful career transition. Such services include counseling, resume assistance, and job placement.

Although advice from family and friends is useful, you may still need professional guidance. Career coaching empowers people to make the right decisions in their professional life, a career coach can guide you to a successful career transition. What are the benefits of having a career coach? Here are three main reasons. Number one, they can hold you accountable. No matter how many times you say to yourself that it's time for a change, but no action has been taken, then expect the time will pass, but nothing will materialize. To avoid wasting your time, energy, and resources you need someone to hold you accountable by meeting up with a career coach on a regular basis, they will remind you if you are on the right path to your goals, by monitoring if you are doing the right steps in reaching your goal. Number two, they can motivate you. Picture this, hundreds of applications, but zero callbacks, frustrating, isn't it?

Obviously, not hearing back from employers can really be a downer for everyone. This is where you need emotional help from a professional, a career coach is your number one source of motivation to keep reaching your goal, their positive remarks and practical advice will invigorate you to keep moving forward. Number three, they can help personalize your career plan. If you've written down your goals, it goes to show that you clearly know what you want to do in life. But the question is, how do you get there, you probably have no idea how and where to start. But this is where a career coach provides the best assistance. They help you identify what exact career you are looking for and will provide a step-by-step plan on how you would achieve it. Oftentimes, they will push you out of your comfort zone, and even schedule informational interviews for you. The point, these professionals can help identify patterns to create a personalized career action plan.

Do not fixate yourself on just one specific job, broaden your horizons. Look at all the career opportunities available to you and create a list. One common way is by asking former colleagues who recently transitioned to new careers. What industries do they move on to, then combine these with jobs that match your interests? Once you find the industry that interests you the most, start immersing yourself in their work culture. Read industry-specific blogs or newsletters, join professional groups in communities and attend networking events.

Another way to assess what career appeals to you the most is by having time to expose yourself to different work fields, in order to get a feel for each area. Try volunteering in different areas of the business, to see if you can become a good fit. Volunteer Match all for good and just serve are one of the top sites to find such volunteering opportunities.

Transitioning to a new career isn't always smooth sailing. In reality, you need to invest time and resources to gain the needed skills to get that dream job. In other words, this may mean going back to school first. After all, you want to make sure that you're fully capable of handling a completely new role. Educating yourself helps improve existing skills or learn new ones.

Fortunately, there are a lot of ways you can learn without technically going back to school. Many colleges and universities offer a plethora of online courses designed to help you learn a new skill or get a new degree with the freedom of flexibility. This helps you to work your way around your schedule with your current responsibilities.

To attract employers to hire you, you need to have a resume that immediately catches their eye. This is why updating resumes is a crucial aspect of applying for jobs that is oftentimes overlooked. Google tips on what to edit on a mid-career resume as well as how to transform it into a powerful career transition resume. Another thing you need to consider is how you create cover letters, when applying for new jobs, generic cover letters are a big no-no. The secret to getting the most callbacks is by creating well-tailored, customized letters. To create a striking cover letter, you should emphasize transferable skills, highlight strong performance in previous positions, and express passion for the company.

Switching gears to a new career doesn't necessarily mean that you need to build a whole new network again from scratch. Inform your friends and colleagues and colleagues about your decision and share with them the details of what you're looking for. They may know someone who has something to offer. In fact, you could even find your dream job with your existing network, without having the hassle of creating new ones in networking events.

Of course, relying on your current network won't be enough to gain the most opportunities. To get the most opportunities, you need to expand your network. Attending networking events in the field you're interested in, is a great medium to build more connections. Prepare an elevator pitch and be confident as you socialize with this new group of people, let everyone know the type of position you're looking for, how it fits with your past work experience. This may seem to be a bit of a stretch, but hey, you'll never know until you try.

When people think about career transition, they often think about moving to a completely new field in a new industry. However, it doesn't always need to be the case, is the new career you're looking for actually available in your current company, why not explore your workplace and see if they may be willing to work with you to make a transition. When you think about it, those people that can help you the most, are the ones that know you the most. Your current management, and since they know your skills and accomplishments, as well as the contributions you've made for the company, they may be more than willing to cooperate and try you out in a new position.

Informational interviews help you to know more information about the career you're pursuing. It's not a job interview. Rather, it's a casual conversation with a person working in a field that you're interested in. Through these informal conversations, you'll get to know what the person's job is like and what it's like working in that industry. To find these people reach out to your existing network, family, friends, and colleagues. If there is a specific company that you're looking to work at, consider messaging employees on LinkedIn, to request an informational interview. You can also consider following up with people you met during networking events. What are the benefits of informational interviews, stress-free conversations, gather inside information, and building relationships?

This is the most crucial part of your career transition. When you want to apply for a new job in a new industry, you'll need to convince the employer during the interview that you have what it takes to take on the new role. How can you prepare well for job interviews? Here are three solid tips. Number one, emphasize relevant skills. The good thing about switching careers is that you don't always have to reset or in other words, start in an entry-level position. With careful preparation, you'll be able to find that dream job. To do that, you need to have a list of specific skills, look for similarities in your original career then highlight them with the job description.

Emphasize the relevant transferable skills that you can bring to the table, one surefire way to attract interviewers, is by highlighting the soft skills, as this is universal. Number two, have a plan for acquiring new skills, even if you're successfully hired for the role, you still need to learn the ropes for this new job. This would most certainly come up in your interview. So, you have to make sure that you're going to dress how you can gain such experience. The common way to do this is by taking a class, finding a mentor, or studying online. However, as mentioned earlier, if you've invested time in learning the new skill in preparation for the job. You can proudly say that you're currently taking classes to improve your knowledge, so you can adjust quickly to your new role. Having this initiative also shows that you're proactive and invested in your new path. Number three, showcase your flexibility. In reality, only a handful of people are hired for a new role, despite the lack of experience. The reason, not everyone deals with change. Well, this is why you need to showcase your flexibility to give employers the confidence to take a chance on you, highlight real-life experiences where you dealt with unexpected changes in your original career, and how you've handled it well professionally.

Look, before you leave, a timeless proverb that reminds us to make sure that everything is alright, before we do something important, especially for life-changing events such as switching careers before you decide to transition to a new career. It would be best if you check your motivations first, ask yourself, why do I really want to switch gears? If you find that work factors such as poor management or toxic coworkers make you want to quit your current job, why not consider changing employers first, maybe we'll start to realize that you're not really tired of your job, you're just tired of the people around you. Another thing to consider is by checking if the root of your unhappiness is actually your job and not a personal issue. When you completely understand why you want to make a change, then you'll be able to make the right decisions.

Finding new work isn't easy, except the hard truth that it might take time for you to find an employer that is willing to take a chance on you. But if you remain confident, enthusiastic and display a positive attitude, you'll eventually find an employer who will provide you that dream job, remaining positive also applies to your journey of taking on the next chapter of your life, rather than dwelling on the negatives of your past employment, use it as a learning experience and keep moving forward.

How do you want your career to be like in the next five years, 10 years, 25 years? More importantly, what can you do to live your life to the fullest. To find the next big thing for you. You need to have a clear vision of your life. For instance, if you want to have a more balanced lifestyle, you might want to consider a career that may pay less than your current job but will allow you to do things that you enjoy the most in life. After all, we work to live, not live to work. On a piece of paper or a blank document, write down your vision and goals, then save it. Or better yet, write it on post-it notes and put it in your office or refrigerator. This serves as a reminder for you, as you pursue this new course. Once you've grabbed that new career, review your vision from time to time. This will help ensure that the path you're taking will always be inclined to your vision.

Everything is on the internet, if you're looking for new career opportunities, then don't miss out on the online world. If you're still using it just for email and social media, then you clearly need to up your game. Increase your online presence by being internet active. If you haven't gotten a LinkedIn account yet, now is the time to join. Update your LinkedIn profile regularly and take advantage of it to connect with people and find new opportunities. Reach out to companies that you're interested in and follow subject matter experts and thought leaders in your preferred niche. Who knows, you may find positions that are more suited for you than what you intend to apply for.

Career transition isn't an impulsive decision, switching careers without proper preparation can lead to professional, and financial setbacks. So, before you set foot on the path to a new journey, you have to ensure that you're ready, financially ready. You do this by means of creating and tracking your personal budget, personal budgeting apps like Mint, YNAB or Quicken help you get a clear picture if you have enough to make both ends meet every month. As I mentioned previously, you may need to apply for online courses to learn a new skill or get a degree or apply for a career coaching session. Expenses such as these should be taken into account during your career transition.

Changing careers can be scary, but fear isn't all bad. Fear helps you to understand how you feel. Identify the negative aspects in your thinking and prepare you for what to do next. But you can use fear in a good way. Turn your anxiety into a powerful tool by practicing this simple exercise. Write down all the fears you have in transitioning careers. For example, you can write something like, I fear that switching careers can be too expensive.

Next, turn each fear into a straightforward question, you can then write, how can I budget my savings for my career change. This process turns your fears into actionable problems that you can then work on, one at a time.

And now it's discussion time. The most important part of this training, whoever's the head honcho with the group should designate a facilitator, whose responsibility it is that each of the questions you see on your screen is covered and that everyone, time permitting, is able to have their say. Make sure all contributions are valued, all suggestions considered, and all opinions respected.

Don't miss out!

Visit the website below and you can sign up to receive emails whenever B. Vincent publishes a new book. There's no charge and no obligation.

https://books2read.com/r/B-A-QWUO-AAKPB

BOOKS 2 READ

Connecting independent readers to independent writers.

Also by B. Vincent

Affiliate Marketing
Affiliate Marketing

Standalone
Affiliate Recruiting
Business Layoffs & Firings
Business and Entrepreneur Guide
Business Remote Workforce
Career Transition

About the Publisher

Accepting manuscripts in the most categories. We love to help people get their words available to the world.

Revival Waves of Glory focus is to provide more options to be published. We do traditional paperbacks, hardcovers, audio books and ebooks all over the world. A traditional royalty-based publisher that offers self-publishing options, Revival Waves provides a very author friendly and transparent publishing process, with President Bill Vincent involved in the full process of your book. Send us your manuscript and we will contact you as soon as possible.

Contact: Bill Vincent at rwgpublishing@yahoo.com www.rwgpublishing.com